I0468210

STUFF for Business (Revisited)

By

Ash Lawrence

www.stuff4business.co.uk

STUFF for Business (Revisited)
Revisited Edition (paperback)
An Aquachain Publishing Book: ISBN-13
9781530281350
Cover Illustration by Dan Lawrence
Additional Cover work Matt Wiley
Cover Photography by Roger Crosby
Internal illustrations by Tym Lawrence
Stuff for Business (Revisited)
Self published by Aquachain August 2014

"Progress is impossible without change, and those who cannot change their minds cannot change anything!"

George Bernard Shaw

Ash Lawrence

Acknowledgements

My Mum, for teaching me my how to manage my emotions.

My Dad, for teaching me to be strong and fight for what I believe in.

My ex-wife, for teaching me that you can't give your all to one thing if you desire another.

My son, Dan, for teaching me that it's more important to be happy than rich.

My son, Adam, for teaching me that rhododendrons are not as important as spending time with your family.

My son, Tom, for teaching me that wisdom isn't restricted to age.

My best mate, for teaching me that true friendship can endure anything.

My lovely wife Sarah, for teaching me to live, love, laugh and be happy. To just be me, truly value myself and above all show me how to be with someone and demonstrate total commitment, trust and unconditional love.

Paul Turner, for introducing me to Dale Carnegie.

Anthony Robbins, for Introducing me to NLP

Everyone I've met for being part of my journey in life.

Foreword

A year ago I attended my first ABC Networking Breakfast. I saw a six-foot four swarthy character looking like someone from a gangster movie. I walked past him in the crowd to get a coffee; he turned from his conversation with several people and said with an easy smile, "You must be Miles." The tough exterior was reinforced by his voice, a kind of posh cockney accent that I associated with someone who could get somebody killed for a bag of cash. Even so, with at least fifty people in the room, did he really know them all that well to spot a newcomer, and remember my name?

And that was the first of many, many surprises since knowing Ash Lawrence. I've always thought myself to be a quick reader of people, but I have ever been updating my view of this guy, and he is nothing that I expected from first impressions (although I can't quite shake the nagging doubt he could organise a hit-man).

So you will find early in this book that Ash doesn't pretend to be something he's not. He speaks as he likes, writes as he likes, and thankfully teaches as he likes. The result is a rough-cut pure diamond. He's nothing like other gurus, and all of us that have met him and attend his Millionaire Mindset Courses, are so glad of it.

Ignore this book, and this man, at your business peril.

Miles Allen
Entrepreneur and Author

Contents

Chapter	Title	Page

"There is none so blind or deaf as the person who thinks they know everything."

Ash Lawrence

Introduction

I attended seven different primary schools, approximately one every six months. I had a teacher that used to smack me on the back of the hand with a ruler telling me that I was the devil's child because I was writing with my left hand.

At eleven years-old I couldn't read or write well enough to even attempt the eleven plus exam, which meant I had go to a secondary school that wasn't my mum and dad's first choice, because my academic level was sub-standard. They thought I was thick!

I left school at sixteen with an O-level in woodwork. I had loads of certificates in running, throwing and kicking or hitting various types and shapes of balls, but nothing of significance on the academic front.

My first real job was in Chatham dockyard as an electrical apprentice; great you might think. For me it was like swapping one set of four walls for another. I lasted nine months.

My mates were labouring on building sites and earning four times the amount I was, so I decided to join them. Luckily my best mate's dad talked me out of that idea and offered me a plumbing and heating apprenticeship.

Not quite as much money, but with the other two part-time jobs I had, it was better than the dockyard, and I could get out of those four walls.

So there I was, seventeen years old, learning to be a plumber by day, moving scaffolding two evenings per week and working on the door for a local night-club Friday and Saturday nights, all for the princely sum of £27-50p.

I was working hard and building relationships.
Two bits of advice I was given, one from my dad and the other from my best mate's dad.

My dad said, *"Son, if you want to get rich you have to work twelve hour days and seven days per week."*

My best mate's dad said, *"It's not just what you know, it's who you know and how well you know them!"* He also said *"Work at the relationships and they will work for you!"*

During the first recession that I can remember in 1990, I decided to move away from the building industry which had served me well. Three young sons a wife and a mortgage and I chose to move into a totally different profession!

I started in the used car trade, believing that if I followed my passion I would be happier as a person, which I was, although, it was like doing an apprenticeship all over again.

It also meant working away from my home and family. The garage I had bought was in Norfolk, and due to the recession we couldn't sell our house in Kent and relocate.

While I was working in Norfolk I was introduced to Paul Turner to whom I am eternally grateful. I instantly liked this man and I couldn't work out why. Six months later I found out.

He invited me over to his house for dinner one evening and during the conversation he introduced me to Dale Carnegie, not personally, although it felt like it, but to his books and courses. This was one of those life-changing moments.

Paul was a Dale Carnegie lecturer and practiced what he preached. The next six months were a massive learning curve for me in building relationships for business and more importantly, life.

Twelve months later I had sold the business in Great Yarmouth and invested in two retail car sales sites in Kent. Worked my arse off for the next seven years building the business, I also added a car, van and minibus hire company, which again I built from scratch.

It was then in 1998 I had another little reminder that things in my life needed to change. I had just arrived home after having a great evening out with my mate and a lovely lady called Stella Artois. I paid the taxi driver and went into make a bacon sandwich as you do after a few too many beers.

While eating I watched a programme on the telly and remember thinking in a drunken haze, *"Wow this bloke is really making sense!"*

Three weeks later I was in my office and the postman turned up with a box. *What's this?* I thought; as I opened it I found an invoice for £196 and a Tony Robbins programme called *"Get the Edge".* How expensive was that drunken night? It really did hit the spot for me, booze and credit cards equal expensive.

That day I travelled to Birmingham to play my national league game of indoor cricket.
I took the tapes with me to play in the car. *(For you youngsters, cassette tapes are what we used to listen to music on!)* I couldn't wait to finish the game and get back in the car and listen to the next tape in the series.

Six months later I exchanged working thirteen out of fourteen days, twelve-hours every day, to working four-hour days, two days per week, and a golf handicap of four. That's how powerful Neuro-Linguistic Programming can be if you integrate it into your whole life.

At this point I thought, *"If I can do that in my business, I can do it for other people's business."*

That was 1999 and I started my journey into self-development working towards a degree in Psychology. Three years later I sold the business and started full-time working with other people and their businesses, helping them make a lot more money with less stress and better lifestyle.

The next ten years saw me attain qualifications as a life and business coach, NLP Practitioner, Master Practitioner and NLP Trainer-Trainer. I studied Cognitive Behavioural Therapy and Emotional Freedom Techniques along with Business and Sports Psychology.

STUFF for Business is my gift to you to help start the change in your life and business that will earn you a lot more money.

However…

"All the knowledge in the world is rendered impotent if it is not followed by ACTION!"

If you are not going to do anything different after reading this book, put it back on the shelf now and save yourself some money.

"One thing is for sure though. If you do put it back on the shelf, it will cost you more money than if you do buy the book!"

"What is impossible to do, but if it could be done, would fundamentally change your business?"

Paradigms, Joel Arthur Baker

My guarantee to you is this:

If after taking action on what you learned in this book, your business isn't better…
-- I'll refund your book fee –

This book isn't for the faint hearted, if you can't face the truth or you don't want to accept total responsibility for you and your successes, then put it down and go and buy something else.

Before you start on STUFF for Business I would like to ask you to do three things for me. Some ground rules if you like…

Ground Rules…

Rule 1- Suspend your Beliefs!

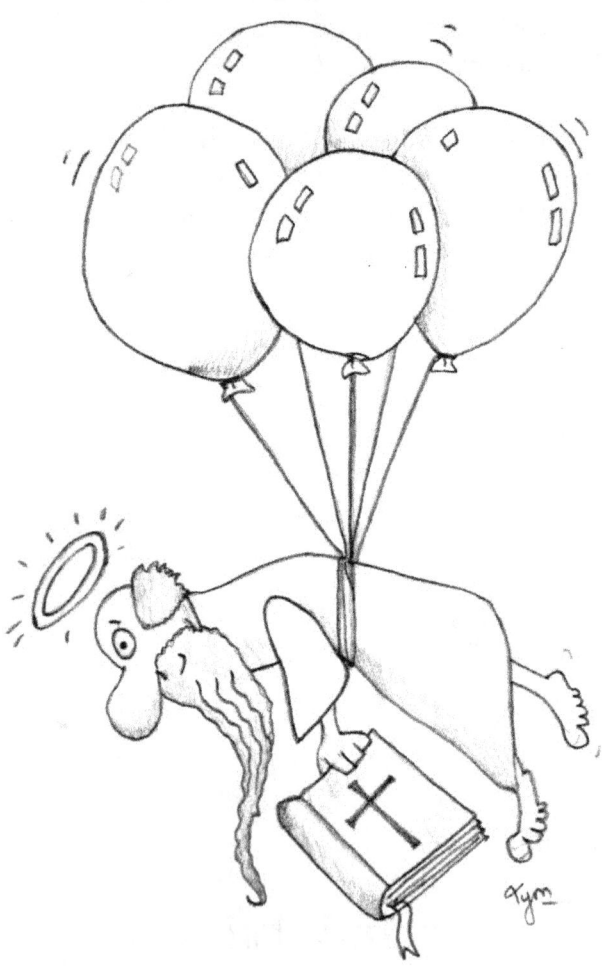

When you go to the cinema to watch a film, do you go in and think, *"That's impossible, that couldn't happen in real life."*

No, of course you don't. What you do is suspend your beliefs for a period of time.

So, that is the first thing I'm asking you to do, suspend your current belief system while you read this book.

Some things may not seem possible to you. They are. I've done them and made a lot of money, and now I'm going to show you how.

Suspend your beliefs, and change your life.

Rule 2- Take Action.

If you don't take action on what you learn in this book, you might as well not read it, so be ready to do at least one of the action points from each chapter. Either you are serious about your business or you're not!

Rule 3- Everything is a choice.

Accept that almost everything in life is a choice, and the very few things we can't choose, we can choose how we think about them.

If you agree to accept the ground rules, I'll set the scene for you…

Please sign your name here that you agree.

…………………………………………………………..
Signed

Content/ Context

I am asked all the time if I could give just one tip for success what would it be. It's a difficult thing to do because it comes down to more than that. It's not industry specific; I wouldn't tell an accountant how to do accounting, a mechanic how to service a car, or a plumber how to fit a bath. It's bigger than that, it's *contextual*.

So what do I mean by contextual?

Imagine there is a meeting between the board of nine directors of a company, and they are deciding which product to go to market with. For the purpose of this exercise imagine the two products are an apple and an orange.

The directors have a vote and are split four for the orange and five for the apple, so they choose the apple. Now imagine, they go to market with the apple and it fails. What are the other four directors who chose orange going to say?

"I told you so!"

If it was the other way round, the other directors would say the same.

So we have to choose in context not in content.

If I said the context for this particular choice was Vitamin C, then all of the directors would have chosen the orange.

Make a decision in Context, then go back and deal with the Content.

One of my clients was a cardboard box manufacturer and was in the process of buying a new machine that automated the process. One was for sale in Holland for £750,000, the other in South Africa for £825,000; both with advantages and disadvantages.

She spent a long time trying to work out which was the right machine to buy. I asked her what was the most important thing for her (Context), and after some deliberation she said, *"Reliability, because if it breaks down it will cost me £50,000 per day."*

So there she had her answer. The one in South Africa, although more money and further away, came with a guarantee that if it went wrong they would fix it within 24 hours and cover her lost earnings.

It's always easier to make a decision in context!
Another thing is, if you take the product out of the business, all businesses are the same. So the tips apply to all businesses and all business people.

Look at the bigger picture, work out what the real issue is then go back and deal with the detail.

I guess that you are proficient in what you do? The world is full of average people and that's perfectly ok, if that's what you want. The fact you are reading this book tells me you want more than average, so you have to *become* more than average.

After many years in business I have come up with five things I believe will stand you out from the crowd and bring success a lot closer to you than it currently is (whatever success might mean to you.)

What I will give you in this book is a formula for success. It will set you on the right lines to make you more money or whatever it is that you haven't currently got, or that which you desire.

However, there is one proviso:

Remember Rule 2

YOU MUST TAKE ACTION!

Action is the only thing that is close to the illusive silver bullet. It's great having a gun full of silver bullets, but if you are not prepared to pull the trigger you might as well throw the gun in the canal.

"The real difference between successful people and unsuccessful people is that successful people take action to make real and lasting change, not just enough to get the job done!"

Successful people achieve success because they have a different Mind-set. In my experience there are two main types of Mind-set:

The *Losers* Mind-set. Is very much of *telling*, *blaming* and *creating excuses* for things that go wrong.

The Winners Mind-set. Is about learning from mistakes and doing it better next time. To Look, Learn, Grow! *More in the next chapter.*

One of the things I have noticed over the years of coaching my employees, people in my seminars and individual clients, is that those who go on to be successful have a mentality of ***Do It Now!***

Some people spend so much time preparing what they are going to do, they miss an opportunity to just do it. Don't worry about getting it right, get it going. Once you get it going it will gain momentum and you can adjust it along the way (you will learn how later in this book).

I've noticed as I visit all of my ABC Networks groups how many people are excellent talkers; they talk a really good game. The reality is that many of them are poor doers.
All talk and no walk.

They have a great theory on how things should be done; they just don't do it themselves, and they remain skint.

Where are you with this talking stuff?
Have you got a story or excuse of why you won't get started, or things not happening in the way you say?
I hear people say, *"I'm a perfectionist and I have to have it right otherwise it drives me crazy."*
Sounds like an excuse not to get going to me!

Most of the entrepreneurs that I know really don't have a lot of patience for thinking about getting going. They have an idea and get on with it; they start the momentum and take action. They **Do It Now!**
So there is your first acronym: **DIN.**
Are you prepared to become a **DIN?**

Some people will say *"I tried my best,"* or *"I'll try and come to your party."* You know as soon as they say *"I'll try"* they won't do what they say they will.
Yoda was right. *"Either do or do not, there is no try!"*

So are you going to take action? If not then put this book back on the shelf, and go and buy a lottery ticket and sit down and watch the telly just like so many others who are not prepared to do what it takes.

There's nothing wrong with that if that's what you *choose* to do, just don't start whinging and whining when good things don't *just happen* for you!
If you have the Losers Mind-set and think that it's *going to go wrong,* it will always go wrong for you.

Things don't just happen; you have to take some ACTION!

Thoughts without action are just dreams. Thoughts with action are dreams come true! It's all a question of belief and choice. What will you choose to believe?

If you take the word "Satisfaction" the last six letters spell action and the word *"Satis"* is Latin for *"enough"*, so together enough ACTION will give you satis f ACTION!

Self-Responsibility...

The last thing we need to sort out before we get onto STUFF for Business is the subject of self-responsibility.

Take responsibility for yourself, nobody is going to save you.

At this point I call your attention to Rule 1. If you want to be successful, you have to take responsibility for everything that happens in your life. Everything! Your income, your debts, your feelings, your thoughts, your health, your weight and your results, with 100% of everything you do and achieve.

I want you to choose to accept complete and total responsibility for everything that happens in your life and remove all blame from your lips.
What is the first thing we do when something goes wrong? We choose something or someone that was the cause - we **BLAME!**

So this is how it works. There can only be three things to blame:

☐ Others
☐ Yourself
☐ Circumstance

Blaming yourself is different from accepting responsibility for a mistake and we will come on to that in a moment.

Too many people say, *"Yeah, it's my fault,"* and of course it might well be their fault. But, it's not whether it's their fault or not, it's about taking responsibility for *their* life.

You can blame others, which is easy to do, and a lot of bosses I've worked with are constantly spending

their time finding someone to blame for the inade-
quacies in the business or with their leadership.

You can blame circumstances, *"I'm not making
enough money because there is a world recession."*

One of my clients a few years back was late for an
appointment with me and phoned to say that he was
an hour behind schedule. When I got to see him that
day he went into a story of why he was late, and this
is how it went:

"I was on my way to work and I had to get some petrol, so I stopped off and filled the car up, went into
pay to find that I didn't have my wallet. I called one
of my managers to get him to come out and pay for
the petrol which put me behind right at the start of
the day.

It was looking like I would be late for my first appointment, so I decided to take the motorway instead
of the back roads. On the motorway I stopped a bit
quick and the car behind me collided with the back
of my car, which made me even later."

So I rewound his day for him like this:

"You had an accident (Others) which made you late.
The reason for the accident was because you went
on the motorway as you were late (Self) and you
thought it would be quicker than going through the
towns.

The reason you were late was because you forgot your wallet (Self). You forgot your wallet because you were rushing since you couldn't find your keys (Self). You couldn't find your keys because you hadn't learnt anything from the previous times you had lost them (Self)."

This is a classic example of not learning from our mistakes and not taking responsibility. The client now puts his keys in the same place when he comes home from work. If he had chosen not to, then he would subconsciously be choosing to lose them.

So it's a choice, either a conscious choice or a sub-conscious choice.

The reason we don't learn from our mistakes is because we have been brought up with the Loser's Mind-set that it's easier to blame something.

From the moment we are born we are dependent on someone else. They provide our food, our comfort, our clothes, our shelter, our education, our money. Everything up to the age of eighteen, someone else is responsible for us. We are *trained* to believe that someone else will step in and save us.

My mum would be constantly saying, "The pools will come up for us this week."

Up until fifteen I thought that some mysterious identical twins were going to drop by and give my mum and dad a million pounds - the brothers, Paul's Littlewoods!

This is where you have to know that, NOBODY is going to save you. There is no magic wand to give you anything, no secret formula to get rich quick. It comes down to YOU accepting responsibility for you and YOUR life and your RESULTS!

The human state is to be in control *(Locus of control)*, and the sad thing is that the moment we blame ourselves, others or circumstance, we give up control over a situation and therefore become a victim.

I can hear you say, *"I'm no victim."*

Well I'm afraid if you are blaming anything, then you most definitely are a victim.

Take responsibility for your life.

Adopt the mantra:

"If it's going to be, then it's up to me."

Instead of blaming someone, yourself or something, ask yourself, *"What can I learn from this situation, how can I get a better result next time?"*

If you make a mistake, work out what you did and how you could do it different next time. A mistake is only a mistake if you make it twice, the first time it is a beautiful lesson.

I'm sure you have heard the term, *"Every cloud has a silver lining."* That's true, in every adversity there is a lesson. The challenge is that most people don't look for it; they go into blame and victim mode.

Let me tell you: every person on this planet, all seven billion of us, has challenges - *all of us.*

The only people without problems are in a grave-yard. The difference is that successful people know this and choose to deal with the challenge; they look for the positive in the situation. Successful people do not BLAME, they DEAL with things.

You have to make the decision to give up your excuses, all of your victim stories of why you haven't got something, or why you can't have something.

Tony Robbins said, *"The only thing stopping people from having what they want is the story they have for why they can't have it."*

You must realise that what you have is the result of the strategy and actions that you have chosen in the past, and that they have been perfect to give you what you have and bring you to where you are.

You have chosen to eat the wrong food that made you fat. The food didn't make you fat, it was the amount and type of food you were putting in your mouth that did that.

You have chosen to spend your money on the things you have bought. If you haven't got enough cash it's because you have chosen to spend more than you earn.

You have chosen a strategy to earn the amount of money that you are currently earning.

I bet you are struggling with that concept!

Take 100% responsibility for where you are and what you have. Stop blaming others for what you have or don't have. Stop blaming for what you feel or don't feel. When you blame others for what you're going through, you deny responsibility and perpetuate the problem.

Stop giving your power away and start taking responsibility for your life. Blaming is just another sorry excuse, and making excuses is the first step towards failure. You and only you are responsible for your life, your choices and your decisions.

It's all a choice and you can choose to look for the silver lining or you can choose to look for the cloud.

Oscar Wilde once said, *"We are all in the gutter; some of us choose to look at the stars."*

It's time to take full responsibility for your life. Be responsible for your choices and mistakes, and be willing to take the necessary steps to improve upon them.

Either you take responsibility for your life and choices or someone else will. When they do, you will become a slave to their ideas and dreams instead of being the maker of your own.

You are the only one who can directly control your life. And no, it may not always be easy. Every person has a whole load of difficult times in front of them. You must take accountability for your situation and overcome these hurdles. Choosing not to, is choosing a lifetime of average existence.

In every situation you have ever been in, positive or negative, the one common thread is you.
Responsibility means recognising that regardless of what happened up to this point in your life, you are capable of making choices to change your situation, or to change the way you think about your situation.
Now you have a choice again. You can either adopt the Loser's mind-set or the Winners mind-set. Find fault and blame, or observe, learn and grow. Which will you choose?

YOUR ATTENTION PLEASE!
No one is coming to save you.
This life of yours is 100% YOUR responsibility.

> *"The streets of the City of Failure are paved with alibis - some of which are absolutely perfect."*

Playwright, Harry Earnshaw

Acton Point...

Your mission from this chapter, should you choose to accept it, is to stop moaning and whinging about why something isn't working for you and turn it into a learning opportunity instead.

Take Responsibility for you.

Remember *"If it's going to be, it's up to me!"*

So prepare yourself for *STUFF for Business*.

It's not for pussies...

STUFF Tip One –*Strategy*

*"If you don't know where you are going,
any road is good enough!"*

Most new business owners start their business with the view they don't want to work for someone else anymore. They may have been made redundant, or just told their boss to stick the job. They leave a regular salary and start off on their own, no long term plan and no vision. They just have a thought that they want to work for themselves from now on. One, two, three years later, or even more, they are broke, depressed and knackered, working harder than they did for their last boss.

One of the problems is - *they didn't have a plan.*

You are just like your satellite navigation system in your car.
What are the two things your satellite navigation needs? It needs to know where you are and where you are going. Successful business owners have their own satellite navigation, knowing both where they are and where they are going.

If what you are doing isn't working, then alter your course to bring you back to *your* target. Readjust your SATNAV and get back on track; make a plan for the future with targets, and start heading towards them.

"If nowhere is your destination then nowhere is where you will end up!"

Successful people focus on what they **can** do about a situation. They take responsibility to change it and they **D**o **I**t **N**ow. The best way to do this is have a plan and take action towards your destination.

Where are you now?

One of the first things the candidates do on my Millionaire Mind-set seminars is to make an accurate assessment of their current position.

What is your exact financial position?
What are your fixed overheads?
What are your variable overheads?
What is your running rate?
How much do you owe, and who to?
What does your product look like in the current market?
What are your competitors doing?
What is your pricing structure?
What does your order book look like?
What is the lifetime value of your clients?

Be honest, don't bullshit yourself.

You need to know your exact position NOW.

The reason you need to know the truth is that an ostrich with its head in the sand means its arse is in the air. That's a very vulnerable position. Accept where you are and do something about it.

If you don't know exactly where you are it's going to be difficult to take the correct action to move forward to where you want to be.

If you are in debt, work out exactly how much you owe and who you owe it to. Pick the phone up and discuss a payment plan with them. Face the facts, you are going to have to pay them at some point so why not discuss a strategy with your debtors and then take action.

If your situation is irretrievable then accept it and make a plan to move forward.

Remember 100% responsibility!

If you haven't got money it's because you have a strategy that is absolutely right to keep you without money. You chose that, no one else.
If your head is full of worry over how you can pay the bills, then you have no room left to think about generating more income, or being creative. You are not moving forward.

Where are you going?

Lots of people have either read a book or been to a seminar on goal setting. They learned to set goals in order to achieve success, and then didn't do them. They choose either consciously or subconsciously not to set goals. If you don't have a goal, how are you going to score?

We are programmed not to set goals from the day we are born. The likelihood is that our parents didn't set goals; they may have had a fluffy dream about winning the football pools or the lottery, but nothing specific and definitive.

Some facts for you;

- 80% of people in the UK do not set goals.
- 15% set goals but don't write them down.
- 3% write them down but don't review them.
- Only 2% write them down and review their goals

So is it a coincidence that only 2% of people earn over £100,000 per year?

If only 2% of people set goals and work to them, the other 98% are destined to work for the 2% that do. If you're not achieving your goals you're achieving someone else's.

Where do you want to be in ten years?

Be specific! If you say, *"I want to be rich"*, that's too ambiguous. Be specific, *"I'm going to have £1,000,000 in the bank 3652 days from today"*.

Visualise the bank statement with that figure in your mind's eye; what would it feel like? What would you hear? Live the complete experience.

What sort of house will you have?
How many rooms?
Where will it be?
What sort of surroundings?
What will your business look like?
How many staff?
What sort of clients will you be working with?
What new products will you have?

Put your complete ten-year vision together, your complete life, all of it!
Now do the same for five, three and one year. **BE SPECIFIC!**

If you aim at the stars and miss, at least you'll land on the moon.
The bigger the vision the better...

Now, let's break it down a little smaller. Where do you need to be in six months, three months, one month, one week, today, in order to achieve your goals? It doesn't matter how you will achieve them at this stage, for now just put together your vision for your business in one, three, five and ten years. If you worry about the how, you'll end up like all of the other business owners that are broke, depressed and knackered.

I was talking to a stranger on the train the other week and the conversation got around to New Year resolutions:

"I don't make new year's resolutions," she said.
"Why not?" I asked.
"They never work out."
"And what do you do differently each year?"
"Nothing," she replied.
"Then why do you expect them to work out if you don't do anything different to make them happen?"
The penny dropped for her. She realised that she had thought about changes, but she hadn't taken any different action.

Every New Year's Eve I take time to formulate my plan for the year ahead. I have a look at what I've achieved in the current year, and then work out exactly what I want to do for the coming year. I bring together all of the new bright ideas too, that I have been writing down through the current year and then, if I haven't already acted on them, include them in a more solid plan for the New Year.

I always have goals, and they are always fluid. They are always on the move, and one thing is for sure, I'm always taking action to move towards them.
You have to set goals, even if they are very small ones to start.

One of the main causes of procrastination is that people set too big a goal, causing their subconscious to believe there is no chance of completing it, so you don't start, you don't take action.
Start today. Start small and make small daily increments.

"The journey of a thousand miles begins with a single step". Lao-tzu

Have the main goal clear in your mind and take small daily steps toward it, focusing on those small steps (covered later in STUFF Tip Three).

Socrates, on being asked by a traveller did he know the way to Mount Olympus, he said, *"Yes, that's easy. Just take a step every day towards Mount Olympus."*

Your ten-year vision may well change along the road, and my experience tells me that it probably won't be anything like it started out. However, it's a great place to start, and remember, if you don't know where you are going, any road is good enough!

What options have you got?

So you know where you are now and you should have a vision of where you want to go. The next step is to investigate the options you have to get you where you want to be.

At this point I find it's down to the quality of questions I ask myself that will determine the results I get.

Here is a selection of questions that I use:
What could I do?
What else?
What could be my first step?
Who else might be able to help?
What would happen if I did nothing?
What has worked for me already?
How could I do more of that?
What do you think others would suggest?
What would happen if I did that?
What is the hardest or most challenging part of that?
What advice would I give to a friend about that?
What would I gain or lose by doing that?
If someone else did that to me, what do I think would happen?
What's the best or worst thing about that option?
Which option do I feel ready to act on?

When you have explored all of your options, ask yourself to come up with just three more things. I know that's really hard, but if you could, what would they be?

Hopefully, you will now have a list of options that you can take action on.

The next step is:

When are you going to do it?

The key point here is to be SPECIFIC.

From the list of your options, which items are you going to do and when are you going to do them? You need to be very specific here.

Again, here is a list of questions you can ask yourself to help make that decision:

How and when will I do that?
What support do I need to get that done?
What do I need from others to help me achieve this?
How will I know when I have done it?
Who will I involve in this?
What would have to happen to know I have achieved the goal?
Who do I need to talk to first?
Who needs to know?
What are three actions I can take now?
On a scale of one to ten, (With ten being ecstatic and one yawning) how excited do you feel about taking these actions?
What would increase that score?
What will happen (what is the cost) of NOT doing this?

With all of that done I must now emphasise that you **GET SPECIFIC**.

Specifically, what are you going to do and specifically when? If you say you are going to start tomorrow, specifically what time tomorrow?

So, you can choose to make a plan, or you can choose to stay broke, depressed and knackered. It's all a choice. Which one will you choose?

Strategy in summary

1. Work out exactly where you are financially. Everything!

2. Make a list of what you want to achieve in ten, five, three and one year's time.

3. Set monthly, weekly and daily goals.

4. What options have you got?

5. What specifically are you going to do?

6. When specifically are you going to do it?

TAKE ACTION
Do It Now
DIN!

"Unless commitment is made, there are only promises and hopes; but no plans."

Management Guru, Peter Drucker

Your mission from **STRATEGY** chapter, should you choose to accept it, is to identify one of your goals from above that doesn't currently have a specific time frame, and commit to completing it by a certain date. Pick a goal that would make the biggest difference to your life if you were to complete it!

STUFF Tip Two -*Trust*

Trust is an underrated and much forgotten aspect of business today. The speed at which you can assess and extend trust determines how fast your business can grow because it affects every relationship.

That is relationships with employees, new staff, business partners, joint venture partners, investors and customers. I expect the subject of trust and its meaning will grow as Facebook, Twitter, Linkedin and other social media sites begins to dictate how consumers are influenced.

Trust is vital to the conduct of business. Some basic level of trust is needed just to have employment contracts, or to engage in any business transaction.
Trust plays a major role.
The level of trust in any relationship, personal or business is more vital to your success than anything else. More so than being great at what you do.

Trust is a two-way relationship; one person trusts, the other is the trusted. While the two are related, they're not the same thing. It is about trustworthiness.

Often we intend more than one thing when we use the word trust. We use it to describe our belief in what people say. We also use it to describe another's behaviour. We use it to describe whether or not we feel comfortable sharing certain information with someone else. We use the same word to indicate whether or not we feel other people have our interests at heart, rather than their own.

If you had to drive to the top of a mountain up a narrow road with a single white line down the middle, just wide enough for two cars to pass, how would you manage to get to the top if you didn't trust the drivers coming towards you to stay on their side of the road?

You wouldn't would you?

So you have to have a level of trust. In this situation, you don't even think about it, you just do. The reason is that the boundaries have been set beforehand; you know that you must not cross the white line.
So you can see that you have to have a predetermined level of trust for things to move forward in most situations.

If you think trust can't be measured on your bottom line, think again. One of the most valuable commodities for any business is time, and if time is wasted it costs money. So if we can save time in our business we can save money, and if we save money it reflects on our bottom line.

Now, it's easy for us to trust someone else, we just choose to trust them.

Easier said than done, perhaps?
Well, let's start with the basics and getting other people to trust us first, shall we?

Make a P.A.C.T. with yourself not with the Devil.

P.A.C.T.

P – Promises!

Have you ever called someone on the telephone for them to say, *"I'm busy, I'll call you back in ten minutes."* And they don't do it? Of course you have, and what's more I bet you have done exactly the same thing.

How did it make you feel? Would you trust them to do what they say next time? If you are like most people, you didn't expect anything different, and therein lays the problem. Everyone has become accustomed to people not doing what they say they will.

So imagine how you will stand out if you do what you say.

How many times have you waited at home for a tradesman to turn up, only to get the phone call to say something has come up and they will be there tomorrow, involving you having more time off?

One of the fastest growing companies in America for two years running was an air conditioning business. They promised that if they didn't turn up within thirty minutes of when they said they would, the customer wouldn't have to pay for the work.

They had to set the specific expectations at the start and they charged about 25% more than other companies, but they did what they said they would do. They cleared up on the business front.

Another example is of a web design company I worked with. They were continually putting back the completion dates of their clients' websites, as seems to be the case with lots of web design companies as I'm sure you may well have experienced yourself.

Once this company started doing exactly what they said they would do they ended up with more business at better prices than most of their competitors, as no other web design company was following through on their promises.

Yes, they had to be quite specific when setting expectations, but that only comes down to *planning*, as we have already discussed. So the first part of building trust with your clients, customers and associates is:

Say what you do, do what you say

.

ALWAYS!

If you can't do it, or there is any doubt, don't say you will. Work out exactly when you can do it and then deliver.

There is too much talk and not enough action from businesses these days. If you start doing what you say, you will clear up as well.

A – Activate Ears!

The second part to building trust is what I call **Activate Ears**. Most of us are too busy thinking about what we are going to say, to be really listening to what is being said. It's called Listening to Respond. We are too busy forming our answer to the agenda that we are running in our own minds.

The car salesman who is thinking to himself, *"How am I going to sell them this car that I have had for sixty days?"* A lot of sales people are guilty of this offence and I'm sure you have experienced that when you have been looking to buy something, the sales person has their own agenda.

Around 93% of divorced women have cited that, "My husband didn't listen to me," as the reason for their divorce.

We need to listen to understand.

Dale Carnegie said, *"Seek first to understand, and then be understood."*

Your task is to really listen to what is being said by the person in front of you, to really find out what they are saying and understand it. Tune into what they are saying, and tune out of the internal dialogue that you have going on in your head.

Active Ears does not mean that you focus only upon what is being said, but also how it is communicated. Communication is between people. Though that may sound like an obvious statement, how often do you carefully read the feelings of the other person communicating?

Quieten your own mind *(tune out),* stop considering what or how you will reply. Instead, really go beyond the sounds, and observe the body language and expressions of the other person *(tune in).* Put yourself in their place.

Study the communicator and you will find out all kinds of insights which will help you better relate to them and avoid misunderstandings.

For instance, what is the other person's preferred style of communication: are they visual, auditory or kinaesthetic?

People with a visual preference will prefer terms like:

- I get the picture.
- I see that now.
- From my perspective.
- What's your view?

People with an auditory preference will prefer terms like:

- I get the message.
- That rings a bell.
- That strikes a chord.
- Sounds okay to me.

People with a kinaesthetic preference will prefer terms like:

- How does that grab you?
- A grasp of the basics.
- It certainly feels right.
- I can relate to that.

How quickly are they speaking?

What is their tone?

All of these things will help you build rapport and their trust in you because they will feel that you are like them, and people like people like them.

C - Compassion

You are not always right! No one is. There are three sides to every story: your side, my side and somewhere in between, is the truth. The trick is accepting that this is the case and then acting on it.

I regularly have lunches to introduce my different clients to each other. One time I introduced a client that owns a charter jet company to another client who is a financial advisor. At the meeting the financial advisor said to the jet guy, *"I have a client at the other end of the country that has two executive jets that he needs to get flying time."*

So the guy with the jets met the other guy with the charter company and started the process of thrashing out a proposal. Neither trusted the other and the negotiations were going on and on, at which point the Financial Advisor asked me to get involved in the capacity of negotiator.

I looked at the situation and worked out the context (common goal) of which they were trying to work together. I put myself in both parties' position and negotiated a deal that suited both parties as I was looking from all sides, not just one.

Those two have now moved on to make a lot of money together and learned a valuable lesson, that there are always three sides to every story.

How could you use that information to build trust? Having empathy for the other person in a dispute or a sales situation is always a great place to be coming from.

It gives you an advantage because the other person probably isn't doing it. You are not always right, even if you think you are.

T – Truth!

Telling lies is not a very good way to build trust. You may get a result in the beginning but it won't last. It's not just about telling lies to others, it's also about the lies you tell to yourself.

"I don't lie to myself," I hear you say. I'm sure that you do and you just don't realise it, and if you do realise it, how stupid are you? Let me give you an example of lying to yourself.

When I was studying to get my qualifications in psychology, I would sometimes sit up until 2am and then go to bed knackered. As I got into bed I would set the alarm for 7am, telling myself that I would get up and go out for a run and then come back, do my press-ups and sit-ups and stretches etc. 7am would come and I would look at the alarm clock and then press the snooze button telling myself just ten more minutes. Ten minutes later I would repeat the process and then again and again until it was 8am and I would finally get out of bed.

The reality is that I was absolutely knackered and needed the sleep and I had lied to myself the night before when I set the alarm, and also every time I pressed the snooze button saying I'd get up in another 10 minutes.

Now when I go to bed I set the alarm for when I will get up. I make the choice between sleep and the exercise, and then when I've made the choice I stick to it. I am truthful to myself, no more little white lies.
When you lie to others or yourself you destroy trust.

There are all sorts of little lies we tell ourselves and others, for instance:

I'm not good enough.
I'll start that diet tomorrow.
I'll start that exercise program tomorrow.
I'll try and come to your party.
I'll call you back in ten minutes.
The cheque is in the post.

And many more little lies just like those.
Do you prefer it if people tell you the truth, or are you happier if they tell you a lie and then just don't follow through on what they have told you?

So you can choose to not trust people or you can choose to set expectations and prepare some systems and processes. It's all a choice.

Which one will you choose?

"Friendship- my definition- is built on two things. Respect and trust. Both elements have to be there. And it has to be mutual. You can have respect for someone, but if you don't have trust, the friendship will crumble."
— <u>Stieg Larsson</u>,

"None of us knows what might happen even the next minute, yet still we go forward. Because we trust. Because we have Faith."
— <u>Paulo Coelho</u>

"You see, you closed your eyes. That was the difference. Sometimes you cannot believe what you see, you have to believe what you feel. And if you are ever going to have other people trust you, you must feel that you can trust them, too--even when you're in the dark. Even when you're falling."
— <u>Mitch Albom</u>

"The best way to find out if you can trust somebody is to trust them."
— <u>Ernest Hemingway</u>

"How would your life be different if...You stopped making negative judgmental assumptions about people you encounter? Let today be the day...You look for the good in everyone you meet and respect their journey."
— <u>Steve Maraboli</u>

Trust in summary
Trust is a two way street.

1. Promises!

(Say what you do, do what you say).

2. Activate Ears!

(Listen to understand, not reply).

3. Compassion!

(Three sides to every story).

4. Truth!

(Especially to yourself).

TAKE ACTION!!
Do It Now!
DIN!

"When you sacrifice your integrity, you erode your most precious leadership possession."

Author, David Cottrell

Your mission from *TRUST* chapter, should you choose to accept it, is to examine where you are not following through on what you say that you will, and start to keep your promises. **ALWAYS!**

STUFF Tip Three -*Unending and Continual Improvement*

I've already shown you that the only way to succeed is to set goals on a regular basis; will you do it? Maybe, for a couple of weeks. Then your subconscious programming would kick back in and you will stop.

So the problem here is your programming.

Earlier you learned that success is very much like a satellite navigation system. You need to know where you are and where you are going. This is where the challenges can start! The way that most of us are set up psychologically is that if the goal is too big we subconsciously turn off because it appears it's too much effort.

Fight or Flight

It is the way our brain is hard wired. We have a little part in out brain called the *Amygdala* which has been part of our brain since prehistoric times. One of the functions of the Amygdala is the *Fight or Flight Response*.

The fight or flight response is a stress reaction that likely evolved out of the survival needs of our early ancestors living with the daily dangers of the time.

Imagine you're a prehistoric caveman (or woman, for the politically correct) relaxing one evening and enjoying your daily catch. Suddenly, a massive, hungry sabre-toothed tiger appears at the entrance to your cave. To him you look like the next meal on his food list, but your subconscious kicks in with a surge of strength and energy, increasing your chances of surviving this encounter. You haven't thought, *"Ah, there is a sabre-toothed tiger, I must run away."* You just reacted and did it.

And so it is in modern days, your conscious mind might say, *"Okay, I'm going to make this big change in my life,"* but the amygdala evokes the subconscious fight or flight in response to the perceived risks of big change, and undermines confidence, so the big change doesn't happen.

This is why most diets don't last, and virtually all New Year resolutions fail after the first month, because the amygdala which controls our subconscious has triggered a defensive response.

So the trick is we have to bypass the amygdala! The way this is done is by small incremental steps on a regular basis that in themselves aren't scary.

Look for small improvements every day!

Kaizen

The process of taking small incremental steps is sometimes called Kaizen, and is the cornerstone of success in your life and business. In Japanese, Kai means small and Zen means change, and together, unending and continual improvement.

When an aeroplane takes off from Gatwick to New York it knows where it is and its planned destination, but for most of the journey it is off target. It is only by a small amount, but it is still off target, and because its destination has been programmed in, the autopilot makes constant small adjustments along the way to keep it on track. It looks at its GPS position and adjusts itself towards its destination. It always knows where it is and where it's going.

So to put Kaizen to work for you it means that you continually check if you are moving towards or away from your target/goal, by making small daily changes. Small thoughts followed by small actions.

Henry Ford once said, *"Nothing is particularly hard if you divide it into small pieces."* The same concept, configured as a question: How do you eat an elephant? Answer: One bite at a time.

This philosophy holds true for achieving your biggest goals. Making small, positive changes like eating a little healthier, exercising a little more, and creating some small productive habits, will achieve them with far greater reliability than any big-bang approach.

And if you start small, you don't need a lot of motivation to get started either. **Do It Now!**

The simple act of getting started and doing something will give you the momentum you need, and soon you'll find yourself in a positive spiral of changes, one building on the other.

Face your problems head-on!

"It isn't your problems that define you, but how you respond to them and recover from them!"

Problems will not disappear unless you take action.

Do what you can, when you can and acknowledge what you've done. It's all about taking small steps in the right direction, inch by inch. These inches count, they add up to yards and yards add up to miles in the long run.

Start with just one activity, and make a plan for how you will deal with troubles when they arise.

For instance, if you're trying to lose weight, come up with a list of healthy snacks you can eat when you get the urge for snacks.

It will be hard in the beginning, but it will get easier. And that's the whole point; as your strength grows you can take on bigger challenges.

You could start by asking yourself small questions like these:

If my health was a priority what small step could I take to make it better? What small exercise could I do every day to add to what I'm already doing? What small thing could I do to remind me to drink more water each day?

How can I save £1 today? If being a millionaire was my main goal what would I be doing right now?

Sowing and Reaping.

You've heard the phrase, *reaping what you sow.* Let me tell you a story that Earl Nightingale used to tell about a farmer and a preacher.

The story goes something like this. A preacher was driving down a country road when he came upon the most beautiful farm he'd ever seen in his lifetime spent travelling rural roads. He could only compare it to a beautiful painting. It was by no means a new farm, but the house and buildings were well constructed and in perfect repair and paint.

A garden around the house was filled with flowers and shrubs. A fine row of trees lined each side of the white gravel drive. The fields were beautifully tilled, and a fine herd of fat dairy cattle grazed knee-deep in the pasture. The site was so arresting, the preacher stopped to drink it all in.

He had been raised on a farm himself, and he knew a great one when he saw it. It was then he noticed the farmer, on a tractor, hard at work, approaching the place where the preacher stood beside his car. When the farmer got closer, the preacher hailed him. The farmer stopped the tractor, turned down the engine and shouted a friendly *"Hello!"* The preacher said to him, *"My good man, God has certainly blessed you with a magnificent farm."*

There was a pause as the farmer took off his cap and shifted in the tractor seat to take a look at his pride and joy. He then looked at the preacher and he said, *"Yes, he has, and we're grateful. But you should have seen this place when He had it all to Himself."*

Well, the preacher looked at the strong, friendly features of the farmer for a moment, smiled, and with a wave of his hand climbed back in his car and continued on his way. And he thought that man has given me my sermon for next Sunday.

Every farmer along this road and in this country has been blessed with the same land, pretty much, and the same opportunity. Each has worked his farm according to his nature. Every farm, every home of every family in the country, is the living reflection of the people who dwell in it.

He understood that the land we're given was not the acres we buy for our farm or the lot on which we build or buy a home, but rather the life we give it, what we do with what we have.

Our lives are our plots of ground, and that's the land we sow, and from which we are obliged to reap the resulting harvest. And the way we've sown will be reflected in every department of our lives.

Well, the farmer that the preacher had just talked to would reap an abundant harvest, not just when the time came for gathering his crops, but every time he looked around the place, every time he returned from town to that white gravel drive and trees that lined it and the fine home and gardens that stood at the end of it. He was grateful for what he had. But he knew that it was not what is given to us that makes the difference, but rather what we do with it, and what we make of what we have.

Yes sir, the preacher thought as he smiled and drove his car along the road to town, I have my sermon for next Sunday, and it will be a good one.

Each one of us is a farmer. Our lives are the plots of ground that have been given to us free and clear. If we're wise, we too, will reap the abundant harvest, for the planting is left strictly to us.

When you sow a thought you can reap an idea. An idea can become an action, an action will have a result, and you can reap the benefits from the result.
So if you want better results, you need to have better thoughts.

So Thought comes first, that thought will lead to an Action, and that action will give us a Result. Thoughts, Action, Result (TAR)

To get better thoughts I use four conscious steps, and for each step I ask, "Is this thought helping me or holding me back?"

1. What am I thinking now?

2. What questions am I asking myself?

3. What experience of the past am I using for referral?

4. What is my future vision of the issue?

For example;

1. What thought am I having?

Ans. *I'm thinking I don't feel like exercising today. Is this helping or holding me back?*

2. I always give up after a while so what's the point?

Ans. *"Is this helping or holding me back?"* It's clearly holding you back so what positive thought could you have? *"If I just exercise for ten minutes, it's better than nothing!"*

3. When I've started to exercise in the past I've always given up and end up putting on even more weight.

Ans. *"Is this helping or holding me back?"* So the positive thought is, *"The past doesn't equal the future, so I'm going to do ten minutes and build up."*

4. I can see myself giving up in six to eight weeks' time.

Ans. *"Is this helping or holding me back? I'm going to imagine being fit and strong and still exercising in one year's time!"*

So you can see that you are training yourself to look for the positive options in every case.

Try it yourself now on a challenge you are facing.

From now on, every time you have a challenge, be consciously aware of asking each of the four questions, and each time also ask, *"Is this thought helping me or holding me back?"*

Inaction

Imagine owning a lovely garden, and part of that garden is a vegetable plot. You prepare the plot and then you have some choices: You can plant something you want to grow; plant something you don't want; or not plant anything at all.

Whatever happens you are guaranteed that *something* will grow. If you planted what you want, you can reap that crop in the future. If you planted something you didn't want you can still reap it, it just won't be the thing you really wanted. You can't plant beans and expect to reap potatoes. If you chose to plant nothing, the ground will still grow weeds.

Inaction will still get a result, it just won't be the result you want. I see a lot of business people that don't take appropriate action and then wonder why they are still struggling to keep their head above water.

I've always lived with the mindset that it's better to make a decision, and that decision be wrong, than not make a decision at all. But if you keep the Kaizen mentality at the front of your thoughts, there's no such thing as a wrong decision, just action and feedback.

If the feedback (the result) isn't what you wanted then change the action! At least you will know by trial and error if you are moving in the right direction.

If you don't take any action in your garden, only weeds will be growing, and your mind has learned nothing. If you don't look after it, it will fill up with weeds. Most people when they leave school give up on all learning unless they have to go on a course for their boss, and then usually under duress.

Take into consideration that if the rate of technological growth is 25% per year, then in four years' time what you know now won't be any good for you.

So if you are serious about being successful you have to constantly invest in your brain. For example, look at how quickly Twitter, LinkedIn, Google and Facebook have grown. Are you fully using social media to grow your business?

Are your competitors?!

What else are you getting behind with?

Think about this; nature's way is: if it's not growing, it's dying. Where are you not growing? What has died off and of no further use to you?

In order for us to grow we often need to let go of other stuff in our life, and that is another bit of Kaizen. You need to clear out things that are no longer any good to you.

Let go of things!

Imagine this, if every time something bad happened to you, you picked up a rock and put it into a rucksack on your back. How long would it be before you couldn't carry it?

Learn to let things go because as you clear out old stuff you create the space for new things to come into your life.

Do it in small pieces, just a little bit every day.

So here's another choice for you. Are you going to take small actions every day to move forward and be successful, or are you going to sit back and let the weeds grow?

Either you want to be successful or you don't.

So you can choose to carry on as you are or you can choose to make small daily changes towards your destination.

"Success is the sum of small efforts, repeated day in and day out."

Robert Collier

"Life is a series of experiences, each of which makes us bigger, even though it is hard to realize this. For the world was built to develop character, and we must learn that the setbacks and griefs which we endure help us in our marching onward."

Henry Ford

Unending and Continual Improvement in Summary

1. Small thoughts and small actions on a daily basis.

2. Ask *"Am I moving towards or away from my goals?"*

3. **T**hought, **A**ction, **R**esult (TAR).

4. Is this thought helping me or holding me back?

5. Plant your garden with the crop you want.

6. Let go of stuff to create space for something new.

TAKE ACTION!!
Do It Now!
DIN!

"In times of change, learners inherit the earth, while the educated who stopped learning find themselves beautifully equipped to deal with a world that no longer exists."

An Anonymous Author

Your mission from **Unending and Continual improvement** chapter, should you choose to accept it, is ask yourself how committed are you to changing your current results? Take control of your learning and commit to learning something new every day.

STUFF Tip Four -*Farming*

Are you a farmer or a hunter? Do you know the difference between farming and hunting in the business world?

It's the difference between relationship selling and transaction selling. Transaction is a one off. Relationship means you can keep coming back and selling other products
.

There is absolutely nothing wrong with hunting the big deal, and one of my clients does that. He sells one aeroplane a year with a commission of £250,000 and that's it. It's a one off transaction.

However, that's just part of his business. He also has a very good relationship style business that he builds off of the back of the transaction business.

It's very much about being aware of the difference between the two.

So let's have a look at what works best for the long term and why.

It's a known fact that people do business with people they like and trust. Your job is to get them to know, like and trust you. This is the basis of relationship selling. Know, like & trust.

In today's market we probably have to make one hundred cold calls to get five appointments, and from the five appointments we will be lucky if we get one sale. I don't know about you, but that sounds like hard work to me.

Also with the economy the way it is, people are being very careful where they are spending their money, and tend to spend it with businesses they have had a pleasant experience with and people they trust.

So how would you like to have close to ten calls, ten appointments and ten sales?
This is how.

Networking

A lot has been said about networking, good and bad. It's very much like Marmite; you either love it or hate it. 95% of my business comes from referrals, and these referrals generally start at a network meeting.

Yes, I know I can hear you say, "It's alright for you as you own your own networking group."
Why do you think I started it?

A lesson I learnt really early on in life was, *"It's not just what you know, it's also who you know, and it's not only who you know, it's how well you know them. More importantly, how well they know you!"*

So yes, it's great building a social network of names on lists.

The real trick is getting to know them in a social situation which builds trust and integrity in you to help you get along in business and life. Networking is no different to belonging to a golf club or the Freemasons or any other group of people that tend to refer work to the people they know, like and trust.

One of my clients, a wealthy and successful financial advisor makes absolutely sure that he meets all of his clients and really gets to know them before he ever talks about business.

He'll go on holiday with them, invite them to come and stay at his house; anything to really get to know them. By doing this he is building a close bond with that person. He is building trust, building respect and building understanding.

So let's get down to successful networking.

If you turn up to a network meeting, hand over your business card and expect a referral, you are getting it wrong. A personal trainer I know turned up to their first ever networking meeting with 50 business cards that he had had printed by a machine in his local shopping centre. He gave one to every person at the meeting, all 27 of them and couldn't understand why he didn't have 27 new clients. He does laugh about this now and is probably today one of the most successful networkers I know.

If you measure your return on investment by counting how many business cards or how much business you got from a particular networking meeting, then you have got it wrong!

Networking is an art form and a process just like any other part of your business. If you haven't had a result from network meetings it's because you haven't had an approach (process) that works.

Plenty of people tend to view it as insincere at best, manipulative at worst. They also reject networking for reasons including lack of self-confidence, fear of rejection and a sense of unworthiness.

If they could just relate to others more easily, if they just possessed more self-confidence and weren't such self-conscious wallflowers the world would be their oyster, and networking would be so much easier.

It is perfectly possible for you, if you are a shrinking violet and shy, to master the skill of networking. You just have to realise that successful networking is all about building sincere relationships based on mutual generosity and trust, not duplicity.

Networking your way to success is a fun and enjoyable process if you want it to be.
If the idea of approaching people you don't know intimidates you, begin your networking efforts by

seeking out familiar faces, such as relatives, friends and current business contacts.

You can do a significant amount of valuable networking without ever having to make a cold call. Starting with a known contact instead of an unknown takes the mystery out of the networking process and helps get a shy person over the hurdle. A series of successful conversations will make you more confident in the method.

Don't apologise!

Introverts and inexperienced networkers tend to apologise when asking for someone's help because they see networking as an imposition, not as an exercise in relationship building. They feel like they're asking someone to do them a favour. They don't think they're worth someone else's time so they start apologising for it.

Apologising just demonstrates a lack of professionalism and confidence. You don't have to apologise for asking for help. You don't have to apologise for wanting to learn more about the individual with whom you're networking. One day you may be able to help them out.

Dale Carnegie's book on networking, *How to Win Friends and Influence People*, which he wrote in 1936, takes the mystery out of networking and gives a process for making friends out of strangers. It also motivated hundreds of business coaches to carry on Carnegie's message.

Here are just a few of Carnegie's suggestions:

Smile:

This is such a simple, basic rule, yet people just don't think about it. They're so focused on needing to network at a meeting they don't realise they're walking around with a face only a mother could love. Angry, serious expressions are forbidding. People are more likely to warm up to someone who says "good morning" with a broad smile than they are to someone with a face like a slapped arse.

Ask open questions:

Joining a group engaged in conversation can feel a little bit awkward if you are a bit shy. The best way to do so is to ask a question to the group after getting the gist of the conversation. You build your credibility by asking a question, and for a shy person, that's a much easier way to engage than by barging in with an opinion.

If you ask a better question you will get a better response. So work out some questions beforehand, like, "How did you get into accounting?"

Listen:

Remember Activate Ears...

One of the most profound points Carnegie made in his book was that people love to talk about themselves. If you can get people to discuss their experiences and opinions - and listen with sincere interest - you can have a great conversation with someone without having to say much at all.

A great way to practice this idea is to go to a party or social situation and don't talk about yourself at all. Every time someone asks about you, think of a way to turn it back onto the other person and find out as much as you can about them. If people ask me what I do, I answer *"I'm a synchronised swimmer, but more importantly, what do you do?"*

Remember, networking is **NOT** about you.

Business cards:

Always have them handy, they are an effective way for you to leave your name behind so that people remember who you are. The rule here is though: don't give them until you are asked! If you ask for their card, they are more than likely to ask for yours.

Make sure your cards are clear, concise and have all of your contact information.

Say the person's name:

People like to hear their own name, pointing to another one of Carnegie's basic principles - *that a person's name is the sweetest sound to that person.* So when you meet someone, use their name in conversation. Doing so makes the other person feel more comfortable, like you really know them and they know you.

Be Yourself:

Many professionals think they have to act like an extrovert or behave in a certain way in networking situations. While you do have to make an effort to be more sociable than normal, you shouldn't be artificial.

You don't have to be a smooth talking Bullshitter. The problem with the Bullshitter's approach to networking is that they don't have the right intent as they are not interested in helping other people, only themselves.

Networking is not about what's in it for you, it's about how can you be of value to others.
Be the authentic, humble, shy person you are. It can be endearing. Just don't try to be something you're not!

Get yourself into different groups:

Just because you're a tradesman doesn't mean you should only go to trades networks. Networking is all about building relationships and that means mixing with as many people as you can. Every social situation is an opportunity to build your list of contacts.

That person sitting next to you on the train, in the pub or at a game of football might have a job you always dreamed about or they might work in a company that you want to get into. You could sit behind them at the game you attend for the whole season and never know that, unless you start a conversation.

"What clubs do you belong to?"
"What are your hobbies?"
"What do you really love doing?"

Attending situations where you feel comfortable helps you put your best foot forward and avoid situations where you might be stressed, rushed or distracted from your networking mission.

When inexperienced people attend network meetings they tend to find one person with whom they spend all their time for the duration of the event. Although settling in with one person may be more comfortable for the network virgin, it defeats the purpose of networking.
If you do know someone at the network meeting, ask them if they could make some introductions on your

behalf. That's a nice soft way for people that are not so confident to meet others.

Nothing to give.

Sometimes people have trouble networking because they don't think they have anything significant, such as a product or a contact, to give back to someone who helped them. Although networking works best when you do have something to offer, what you offer doesn't have to be something for sale.

Sincere interest in the other person, even flattery, is a form of generosity and goes a long way when you're networking. Just be you, share your passions and help other people feel good or be more successful, that's all you have to do to network. Remember the primary reason you are networking is to build relationships. You are sowing now to reap later!
Remember: Know, Like & Trust.

Freezing-up

If you're afraid you'll freeze up or get tongue-tied in a social setting, prepare yourself in advance. Think of open ended questions you can ask people you meet. If you're attending a regular network event to promote your business, have your personal pitch ready.
Your pitch needs to have a basic 5 elements;

- Why you're worth listening to.
- What challenge you are fixing.
- What will happen if they don't fix it.
- What have you got to fix it.
- What social proof do you have.

Anticipate questions you may be asked, such as what you do, and have clear, concise answers at the ready. Your delivery has to be attention grabbing to overcome interruptions and compensate for a lack of privacy.

Don't be boring.

I've been to so many networking events where people stand up to give their one minute pitch and start with their name and occupation. The problem with this is that psychologically 25% of the room turn off at your name and a further 50% turn off when they hear your occupation.

So if you are lucky you may have 25% of the people listening. That 25% will also dwindle if there has been another person in your trade or profession talk before you.

If you're just talking about what you do then you could only have 5% of the room listening. The trick here is to start with an attention grabber! I tend to tell interesting stories about anything other than psychology or my Mind-set seminars. After all, we don't want to bore them before we start!

For example:

"Good morning, years ago Tolstoy used to tell a story to his children about the secret of everlasting happiness, and I'm sure you would all like to know that particular secret? He said that if they truly *wanted to find the secret of everlasting happiness it was really easy and was in their own back yard! The only thing that they had to do, when they went to look for it, was they mustn't think about white rabbits. Of course they remembered that, and when they went in search in their back garden they reminded themselves that they mustn't think about the white rabbits, and in order not to think about it they inadvertently did. So, they never did find everlasting happiness. My name is Ash Lawrence, and if you want to know how to beat the white rabbit syndrome, come and have a chat."*

It's not how you start; *it's how you finish*.

The last thing you do is say your name and occupation, that way it's more likely to stay in everyone's mind.

"**When you are networking, people will prefer a metaphor to a sales pitch.**"

Update your database!

So now you've done all that work and found out about the people that you have met. The next step is to add all of the information to your database or customer relationship Manager (CRM): Outlook, LinkedIn, Twitter and Facebook accounts.

That's another tip, if you haven't got LinkedIn, Twitter and Facebook, get it sorted.
If you're a novice then it's well worth the time and money going to a workshop on social media for business to get started.

Whether you like it or whether you don't, the first thing people do these days is pick up their phone and look for you on Linkedin, Facebook or Twitter and if they can't find you they will move onto the next person that they can.

Keeping track of your connections and maintaining your relationship with people is a vital part of networking. There are lots of ways you can keep track of your network. Some people like to keep files full of business cards, others store their contacts in Outlook or rely on online networks like I've mentioned earlier.

The way you choose to keep track of your contacts isn't important. The important thing is that you do it, and that you periodically catch up with each one of your contacts to avoid losing touch. I always send an email to any new people I have met just thanking them for taking the time to talk to me and saying how great it was to meet them.

This simple act can mean the difference between the relationship lasting, and never hearing from them again. It is also shows that you are thinking about them, and additionally, if they didn't take your business card it gives them your details for future reference.

This is such an important point that I really can't stress it enough.

Why go to all the effort of going to a network meeting, finding and starting a conversation with a new contact, only to run the risk of never hearing from them again because you didn't follow up?

It's great to spend time at a networking event with someone you know and like. But that's not what you're there for. Your goal is to expand your network by meeting new people.

Lead generation is a major part of any business, and networking is probably the best lead generation method for relationship style businesses.

My philosophy for networking is to *"Turn strangers into friends, and friends into clients!"*

"You can close more business in two months by becoming interested in other people than you can in two years by trying to get people interested in you!"
Dale Carnegie

So you can choose to be a hunter or you can choose to be a farmer.
Which will it be?

If you want 1 year of prosperity, grow grain. If you want 10 years of prosperity, grow trees. If you want 100 years of prosperity, grow people. Chinese Proverb

Farming in summary

1. Get yourself booked into a local network meeting.

2. Circulate and meet NEW people.

3. Remember the focus isn't on you.

4. Ask open questions, listen and be genuinely interested in the response.

5. Ask for their business card. Do not offer yours unless asked for.

6. Sort out your one-minute pitch!

7. Tell a story.

TAKE ACTION
Do It Now
DIN!

"Try not to become a man of success, but rather try to become a man of value."

Albert Einstein

Your mission from *FARMING* chapter, if you choose to accept it, is to contact one of your customers, clients or network contacts regarding something other than your product or service to add value to their lives!

STUFF Tip Five -*Fun*

The power of having fun at work should never be underestimated. People are simply more productive and motivated if they are having fun. It's just the way we are wired.

If we look at children, we would see that they learn best when they are playing. Playing is also the best way of motivating them to do something. The sad thing is, as we grow up and progress further in life, we eliminate the fun element. We get all serious.

Sod that for a game of soldiers!

No wonder humans learn the most in their first five years of their lives. Everyone, and I mean everyone, has a child inside of him or her that wants to come out to play. It's part of who we are and it shouldn't be any different at work.

In years gone by people used to believe that fun is something that starts on a Friday afternoon and ends on Sunday evening, or at a conference or a party. It certainly isn't something they associate with work. Today people want and need to have fun WHILE they are working, right through from Monday to Friday.

If you have fun at work you will never work another day in your life.

Happiness Formula

Most people believe that success is the route to happiness, that if you are successful you will be happy. The contrary is actually true. Happiness is the route to success. If you are happy then you are actually successful.

I know that may cause some cognitive dissonance for you so let's see what we can do about that.

In 1543 Nicholas Copernicus revealed to the world that the earth revolved around the sun not the other way round. For all those years we humans had a belief that was incorrect.
Today we have now discovered that happiness doesn't revolve around success; that too, is the other way around.

Happiness comes before success.

For years we have been taught that in order to be happy we must be successful, to have that new car, to have that Rolex, to get that pay rise, to have whatever the new stuff on the market is. Well, let me tell you, that kind of thinking is incorrect also, it's back to front.
Take a moment and consider this! Your life up until now has been striving for happiness as something that is out there, waiting for you to get everything you want then you will be happy.

I'm going to invoke Rule 1 again and ask you to suspend your belief for a little longer.

Imagine you could be totally happy just by thinking about being happy. How would that make you feel right now? Happy of course! Happiness is just a feeling, and like every other feeling they all come from thoughts.

T.E.A.R.

Remember earlier in this book, Thoughts, Action, Results? Well, now I'm taking it up a notch.

Thoughts-**E**motions-**A**ction-**R**esults.

Another acronym, *TEAR!* We can think our emotions!

One of the exercises I get my clients to do is think of a song that makes them sad, play it in their head, get them to feel the sad song. Next I ask them to think of a song that makes them feel happy, then imagine the song, get the lyrics or the beat into their being.

So, in the space of about 45 seconds they have gone from sad to happy. The only thing that has changed was the way they felt, and they did that by thinking about it.

Try it yourself now!

Hopefully, you have now connected thoughts with emotions and realised that it is the thoughts that create the emotions and not the actual event.

It's not the event that makes you sad, but the meaning you attach to the event. This is called a *learned behaviour*.

We learn all sorts of different emotions and how to connect that emotion to an event.

Let me give you an example; you have a friend and they decide to go touring on the other side of the world. You don't hear from them for a whole year, and then you get news that they died. You are understandably upset.

The question is; are you upset with the event or the meaning you have attached to the event?

You then go on to find out that they actually died on the first day of their holiday which is one year ago. So you are not upset with the event, you are upset with the meaning that you have attached to that particular event.

Is it hard for you to accept that bit?

Let me break it down a bit for you. The event was 365 days ago, so you had no idea that it happened then. So you were not upset on the day they died *(the event)* you were only upset when you heard about it and then started to think about the event and the consequences, along the lines of, I wonder how it happened? Were they in pain? I won't be able to talk to them again. And so on.

You were having a conditioned response based on a learnt behaviour or an expected behaviour in a certain set of circumstances. So it was the thoughts you created about the event that actually evoked the feelings. Thoughts create feelings.

Another example of learned emotion is fear. We are born with only two fears, which are falling and loud noise. All of the others are learned. We weren't born afraid of clowns, and now we are. We learned that from other people! So if we can learn them, we can unlearn them.

Ok, so that's the serious part out of the way, let's move on to the fun stuff. We are happier if we are having fun at whatever we do because, if we are having fun it means we are enjoying what we do, and if we are enjoying what we do it doesn't feel like work.

If you are currently not enjoying what you do, change what you do, or change the way you think about it.

Focus...

The problem is that a lot of people in business are so wrapped up in the day to day events and problems that they don't really enjoy what they are doing, so having fun isn't an option for them. We all have problems, remember. The only people without adversity in their life are in the graveyard. The real difference between happy people and unhappy people is the way they deal with their adversity.

Staying in the present moment is a great way to start the happiness process.

Many of our negative thoughts come from worrying about situations that never happen. While you may often have to make contingency plans, constantly thinking about the worst case scenario can place undue stress on your mind and body and drain it of energy that could be better used in more productive things.

If you focus on what you can do now, instead of what may or may not happen, you are more likely to find the resource to deal with the challenge at hand.
This also applies to having fun with what you are doing, whatever that may be. Tune in to what you like about what you are doing instead of tuning into what you don't like. Appreciate the here and now. Stay present!

Right now is a miracle.
Right now is the only moment guaranteed to you.
Right now is life. So stop thinking about how great things will be in the future. Stop dwelling on what did or didn't happen in the past.

Learn to be in the *here and now* and experience life as its happening. Appreciate the world for the beauty that it holds, right now!

Positive versus Negative!

Engage in positive thinking. Shifting negative thoughts to positive ones will help to improve your mood. Research suggests that positive people are smarter than negative people!
I'm invoking Rule 1 again here. Suspend your belief and open your mind to what might be, instead of what you think you know.

I hear people say, "Positive thinking is ok for dreamers and not realists." Well that hasn't always been the case.

When we think positive we release the endorphins serotonin and dopamine into our brain which has been proven to expand our neurotransmitters and make us slightly more intelligent. Not a lot, but enough to make a difference.

Ash Lawrence

The best way to deal with negative thoughts is to separate fact from fiction. So, the next time you find yourself having a negative thought, have a look at the situation and ask whether you're reacting to a real or imagined situation. Is this thought helping me, or holding me back?

Research also suggests that negativity is three times more powerful than positivity which just goes to show how negativity holds you back. So if you have one negative thought you have to replace it with three positive thoughts. People in depression focus on the negative and therefore send themselves into an ever declining spiral.

The mind must believe it **CAN** do something before it is capable of actually doing it. The way to overcome negative thoughts and destructive emotions is to develop opposing, positive emotions that are stronger and more powerful.

Listen to your self-talk and replace negative thoughts with positive ones. Regardless of how a situation seems, focus on what you **DO** want to happen, and then take the next positive step forward.

Life gets better when you choose to make it better. Negative people make lots of noise about how bad things are, while positive people quietly and steadily improve things. There are always problems, there are always challenges, and there are always people willing to transform those problems and challenges into great opportunities. Those who have the courage, commitment and discipline to do so, create a better life for everyone.

Be one of these people...

Focus on solutions not problems and work your way positively towards a brighter future. You can't control everything that happens to you, but you can control how you respond to things. Everyone's life has positive and negative aspects. Whether or not you're happy and successful in the long run depends greatly on which aspects you focus on.

Every time a negative thought comes into your head, stop and think about three positive ones. Do this for a few weeks and you'll quickly notice that you're creating a new habit that will improve your happiness at every level in your life.

Worst case scenario is that in the end the pessimist may occasionally be proved right, but the optimist has had a better time in the process!

Helping Others...

Helping others, whether getting involved in charitable activities or helping other people in general, is one of the secrets to everlasting happiness.

Happiness at work isn't about what you achieve on your own. It's not about you, remember? Giving is better than receiving. Think about what you can do for your society rather than what your society can do for you.

Only do what you can...

While you may often believe that you are motivated by being under pressure, the kind of pressure that pushes us to do more, it's important to notice when your mind and body need a break.

Even if you love what you do, pressure can weigh you down and make you unhappy. Plan a few days off or find an outlet after work or at the weekend to have fun, rest your mind and rejuvenate yourself. Offer to help work with a charity or contribute in some other way.

Maintain an Attitude of Gratitude...

Happiness doesn't come from getting something you don't have; it does come from recognising and appreciating what you do have. Write down five things you're grateful for each day before you start work, or before you leave the office at the end of the day, to retrain your brain to focus on the positive.

If you are continually focusing on what you want instead of what you have you are setting yourself up for failure. It's not about having what you want; it's about wanting what you have!

Researchers have found that people who want more of what they have tend to be happier than those who want less of what they have, and people who have more of what they want tend to be happier than those who have less of what they want. Remember that what you have today you once longed for yesterday.

If it made you happy for a few minutes, hours or days and it doesn't make you happy now, ask yourself why what you are hankering after now will make you happier for any longer than the last thing you wanted?

If you are waiting for someone else to make you happy, you're missing out. Smile because you can.

Choose happiness...

Be the change you want to see in the world. Be happy with who you are now, and let your positivity inspire your journey into the future.

Happiness is often found when and where you decide to look for it. If you look for happiness within the opportunities you have, you will eventually find it. But if you constantly look for something else, unfortunately, you'll find that too!

An oyster may look like a grubby crustacean on the outside, on the inside there is a beautiful pearl.
When things are hard, and you feel down, take a few deep breaths and look for the pearl – that glimmer of liberation.

Remind yourself that you can and will grow stronger from these hard times. And remain conscious of your blessings and victories, all the things in your life that are right. Focus on what you have, not on what you haven't.

Look for the pearl!

There will be a pearl; you just have to look for it.

So you can choose to look for the pearl or you can choose to smell the manure, which will it be?

Fun in summary

1. Happiness before success.

2. **T**hought **E**motion **A**ction **R**esult (TEAR).

3. Stay in the present moment.

4. Engage in positive thinking.

5. Help others.

6. Maintain an Attitude of Gratitude.

7. Look for the pearl.

TAKE ACTION
Do It Now
DIN!

"I honestly think it is better to be a failure at something you love than to be a success at something you hate."

Comedian, George Burns

Your mission for the *FUN* chapter, should you choose to accept it, is to reflect on how you feel about what you do for a living. If you are not enjoying it, find a way to change it. Life is too short to be unhappy.

Stuff for Business – In short for your referral!

Tip One – *Strategy!*

1. Work out exactly where you are financially-Everything!
2. Make a list of what you want to achieve in ten, five, three, one year's time.
3. Set monthly, weekly and daily goals. Be specific.
4. Visualise it, feel it, hear it. Make it real in your mind!

Tip Two – *Trust!*

1. Make a **PACT** with yourself:
2. **P**romises (Say what you do, do what you say).
3. **A**ctivate Ears! (Listen to understand, not reply).
4. **C**ompassion (three sides to every story).
5. **T**ruth (especially to yourself).

Tip Three - *Unending continual improvement!*

1. Small thoughts and small actions.
2. Towards or away?
3. Thought, Action, Result (TAR).
4. Is this thought helping me or holding me back?
5. Plant your garden with the crop you want.
6. Let go of stuff to create space for something new.

Tip Four – *Farming!*

1. Get yourself booked into a local network meeting.
2. Circulate.
3. Remember the focus isn't on you.
4. Ask questions and be genuinely interested in the response.
5. Ask for their business card. Do not offer yours unless asked for.
6. Sort out your one minute pitch! Tell a story.

Tip Five – *Fun!*

1. Happiness before success.
2. Thought, Emotion, Action, Result (TEAR)
3. Stay in the present moment.
4. Engage in positive thinking.
5. Help others.
6. Have some fun.
7. Maintain an Attitude of Gratitude

TAKE ACTION
Do It Now
DIN!

My Greatest Lesson

"The quality of your life is directly proportional to the quality of your relationships, and the quality of your relationships is directly proportional to the quality of your communication. If you want a great life, learn how to communicate at the highest level."

Ash Lawrence...

Extras

Suggested reading list

The Go Giver - *Bob Burg*

Go Givers Sell More - *Bob Burg*

Endless Referrals - *Bob Burg*

How To Win Friends And
Influence People - *Dale Carnegie*

The Inner Game of Selling - *Ron Whillingham*

Eat That Frog - *Brian Tracy*

Key Person of Influence *Daniel Priestly*

The Entrepreneur Revolution *Daniel Priestly*

Psycho-Cybernetics *Maxwell Maltz*

Testimonials from Stuff for Business!

Just have a read of what some of the people that bought the original Stuff for Business have said;

I have read many books in my 16 years in network marketing.
Some, of course, have proved to be of greater value than others. I must say that "Stuff for Business" by Ash Lawrence really hits the spot. It's straight talking, no nonsense approach is just what the doctor ordered!!
It is an easy read and contains simple action plans at the end of each chapter. A lot of my team members now have the book and we are all moving forward and living our lives ON PURPOSE! Thank you Ash. **Sue Boswell.**

Never thought I would read a book as I normally take for ever, but after the first few pages I could not put the book down, so many good ideas and true words, just think the impossible and open your mind and who knows where you could go in your Business. Just get the Book DIN! **Chris Verbiest.**

Ash's take on business is like no other, by following the "instructions" contained I have completely restructured my business and the results have been unbelievable. Easy to read with no mumbo-jumbo language to get through, this is the best money you will ever spend on your personal growth. This has gone in to the top 5 books I've ever read. As Ash would say, "get it, and get it now!" **Martin Doyle**

STUFF is a fantastic book. It works very much on the K.I.S.S principle and as such is an easy to read and implement guide to business.
Well done, Ash...I look forward to the next one. **Tim Box**

People said 'Ah sure you'll read it over two days.' That was not my wish- I wanted to take my time and savour and absorb this re fresher on how to have more success and results in business. Congrats Ash you nailed it- straight and to the point.

This book is essential reading for people not just in business, it is also a must read for everyone. It covers how we can change and live successfully in every aspect of our daily lives too.
Read it, use it and never lose it. Thank you Ash....
Continued Success **Miriam McGuirk**

I bought STUFF for Business as I really thought it would help me with my business, had I know that my husband was going to pinch it and read it first I would have bought him his own copy.

The book has inspired our whole family and we actively use it in everyday life, and when I'm a little stuck I can either refer back to the book for more guidance, or talk to my husband about it, as he has read the book too he often quotes bits to me from the book, sometimes its better to be able to share things in business with your partners, and out of the gazillions of books we've read over the years, this one is by far my favourite.

If you're serious about your business - buy the book **Trayc Randall**

The best thing that ever happened to me was to be recommended to and introduced to Ash Lawrence, by a close friend, this book is inspirational and reinforces what I have learnt on the millionaire mind-set course that Ash teaches.
I have been in business for 10 years and I was skint depressed and Knackered, signing up for the course I am know 7 months in and have turning my business around being so worried about networking but realising the people you meet are all kind and ABC is like a big family. I am thankful every day that I met Ash and Sarah Lawrence, the book is a great read and I highly recommend the course Ash delivers no nonsense straight to the point no excuses. If you're serious about your business and want to earn more cash Talk to Ash. **Lesley Holloway**

Have read a lot of great quality business books in the last year and this is my favourite. They all share a message that they are nothing without the application and this was by far the one that just 'clicked' it all into place for me.
Great content delivered well and has made a vast increase in my networking, business acumen and sales.
A must have. **Ross Cowan**

Please feel free to connect with me…

Ash Lawrence
http://www.facebook.com/ashmindset
www.twitter.com/@ashmindset
http://www.linkedin.com/in/aquachain
www.ashlawrence.co.uk
http://blog.ashlawrence.co.uk/
ABC Networks
www.abcnetworks.co.uk
www.facebook.com/ABCNetworks
www.twitter.com/@ABC_Networks

Books also by me….

Wily Old Fox Wisdom…

Coming Soon…

Soft STUFF for business…

Would you like to take your business to the next level? Then try Ash's **E**ntrepreneurs **B**usiness **C**lub.

www.ashlawrence.co.uk/seminars